Original title:
When I Let Go

Copyright © 2024 Swan Charm
All rights reserved.

Author: Linda Leevike
ISBN HARDBACK: 978-9916-89-703-4
ISBN PAPERBACK: 978-9916-89-704-1
ISBN EBOOK: 978-9916-89-705-8

The Light Within Set Free

In the silence of the heart, a spark,
A flicker bright, dispelling dark.
With faith and hope, it starts to grow,
A radiant light, a sacred glow.

Whispers of truth, gentle and clear,
Calling us forth, to draw us near.
With every breath, let the spirit soar,
Unleashing love forevermore.

The chains of doubt begin to break,
As we embrace the path we make.
In unity, we rise above,
Empowered by the grace of love.

The light within, a guiding fire,
Ignites the soul with holy desire.
In surrender, we find our peace,
A journey of faith that will not cease.

Embrace the light, let it lead,
In every heart, plant the seed.
For in the depths of all we see,
Lies the sacred truth, set free.

The Unseen Guiding Hand

In shadows deep where fears may dwell,
An unseen hand begins to swell.
With gentle touch, the heart is stirred,
A whispering voice, a guiding word.

Through trials faced and mountains high,
We find our strength, we learn to fly.
With every step, the path unfolds,
The story of grace, forever told.

In moments still, we feel the grace,
A guiding presence, a warm embrace.
With every doubt, a light appears,
Dispelling darkness, calming fears.

The unseen hand, a source of might,
Illuminates the darkest night.
Through storm and strife, we learn to trust,
In love divine, we rise, we must.

So take a breath, and let it be,
The guiding hand will set you free.
In faith we walk, in love we stand,
Forever held by the unseen hand.

In the Quiet Embrace

In silence, He listens, a tender breath,
With whispers of peace, He conquers death.
In shadows of doubt, His light remains,
A refuge of love through all our pains.

In moments of sorrow, He draws us near,
A balm for our wounds, dispelling fear.
With hands extended, He gently holds,
In the quiet embrace, true love unfolds.

The Grace of Release

In burdens we carry, His kindness flows,
With every release, His mercy glows.
Chains of the past, we shed with prayer,
In the grace of release, we find our air.

The weight of our sins upon Him laid,
In humility's light, our hearts are made.
Forgiveness blooms where sorrow wanes,
In His loving kindness, our freedom gains.

Faithful Steps into the Unknown

With each step forward, we tread in faith,
In paths uncharted, we find our place.
Though fear may linger, our hearts are bold,
In His promise of love, we break the mold.

Through valleys of doubt, we journey on,
In shadows that whisper, His truth's a dawn.
With every heartbeat, His guidance flows,
As faithful steps lead where grace bestows.

The Benevolent Unbinding

In love's gentle hands, we find release,
The shackles of worry, a path to peace.
The ties that once bound us break with trust,
In the benevolent unbinding, we rise from dust.

With eyes uplifted, our spirits soar,
In the light of His love, we seek no more.
As chains of despair are cast away,
In freedom's embrace, we find our way.

The Faithful Letting Loose

In the quiet hours of night,
Hearts lift in sacred flight.
Songs of praise softly rise,
Whispers dance 'neath starry skies.

Embraced by love divine,
Joy flows like sweetened wine.
Graces pour from heaven's flow,
In faith, we learn to grow.

Every burden cast away,
We rejoice in endless play.
Spirit's light ignites our core,
In unity, we soar.

Through trials, we stand tall,
In His name, we give our all.
With open hearts, we proclaim,
In His truth, we find our flame.

Gentle hands lift us high,
On wings of prayer, we fly.
With faithful hearts, we entwine,
In His love, we forever shine.

Epiphany in the Evening Breeze

As the sun dips low and fades,
Soft whispers drift through glades.
In twilight's gentle embrace,
We find our sacred place.

The breeze carries thoughts so pure,
Revelations, we are sure.
Light breaks forth within our soul,
In His presence, we feel whole.

Stars emerge, a heavenly sight,
Guiding us through the night.
In stillness, our fears cease,
We surrender, find our peace.

With every breath, we connect,
In His love, we reflect.
Truth unfurls, gentle and kind,
In the night, we seek and find.

Each moment, a chance to see,
The beauty of what can be.
As darkness gives way to grace,
We emerge, hearts in place.

Offering the Weight to Heaven

With burdens heavy on our chest,
We seek solace, find our rest.
In the silence, voices blend,
Hands uplifted, hearts extend.

Every tear, a sacred stream,
In His arms, we dare to dream.
Offerings of pain and strife,
Transforming darkness into life.

Faithful hearts pour forth their plea,
In surrender, we are free.
Casting worries to the skies,
In His mercy, our hope lies.

The weight released, a sweet embrace,
With gratitude, we find our place.
In letting go, we find a way,
To live in love, come what may.

Together, we rise above,
A community bound in love.
Offering our weight, we learn,
In His light, we brightly burn.

The Spirit's Gentle Release

In the stillness of the morn,
A dawn of hope is reborn.
The Spirit's whispers softly call,
Inviting us to rise and stand tall.

In every thought and gentle sigh,
We sense His comfort drawing nigh.
Breath of life, breathe through me,
In this moment, I am free.

Letting go of chains that bind,
Finding freedom in His kind.
The weight of worries drifts away,
As love guides us through the day.

With every heartbeat, peace unfolds,
A tale of grace, forever told.
In the light of faith we trust,
In His love, we rise and adjust.

The Spirit's touch, a gentle flow,
In His presence, we learn to grow.
Embracing all that life may bring,
In joyful praise, our hearts will sing.

Faith's Gentle Departure

In twilight's glow, the heart finds peace,
Trust in the journey, sweet release.
Each whispering prayer, a guiding light,
Beneath the stars, through endless night.

The soul arises, fears unspun,
With grace it dances, knows the sun.
Let go of burdens, softly tread,
In faith's embrace, all doubts are shed.

Through trials faced, through love bestowed,
The spirit thrives on this winding road.
In sacred moments, wisdom flows,
The seeds of hope, the heart now knows.

As shadows wane and spirits rise,
In solace found, beneath broad skies.
For every tear, a bloom shall grow,
In faith's departure, we learn to glow.

The Solace of Untethering

In quiet grace, we slip the binds,
A gentle breeze, where love reminds.
The heart unchained, begins to soar,
In untethered dreams, we seek for more.

With every step, the world expands,
In faith's horizon, love commands.
Release the fears that weigh us down,
In joyful trust, no need to drown.

The light within begins to bloom,
In sacred spaces, we dispel gloom.
With open hearts, we find our way,
Embracing dawn, we greet the day.

In every moment, a breath divine,
In kindness shared, our spirits shine.
In untethering, the soul takes flight,
The solace found in purest light.

In Divine Hands

With every heartbeat, stillness flows,
In divine hands, our spirit knows.
Through trials faced, we learn to bend,
Trusting the path that has no end.

In whispered prayers, we seek the peace,
With hope and love, our fears release.
Each moment cherished, held so tight,
In divine hands, we find the light.

The journey winds, yet we stand strong,
In faith's embrace, we all belong.
Through pain and joy, we learn to sing,
In divine hands, we find our wings.

As shadows fade, and dawn appears,
We gather courage, release our fears.
With hearts united, we shall ascend,
In divine hands, love has no end.

Serene Surrender

In quietude, we breathe in trust,
Serene surrender, our souls adjust.
With each exhale, we let things be,
In stillness found, we learn to see.

The world around, a canvas bright,
In colors bold, we find the light.
With open arms, we embrace the flow,
In serene surrender, our spirits grow.

When storms may rise, and shadows fall,
We find our peace, answering the call.
In surrender's strength, we find our truth,
With heart and faith, we shine our youth.

The universe whispers, guides our way,
In fragrant blooms of each new day.
In serene surrender, joy doth take root,
As love's sweet melody calls us, astute.

The Whisper of Letting Be

In stillness, a gentle breeze flows,
Softly echoing the heart's repose.
In shadows, truth begins to gleam,
Letting go, we find the dream.

A voice within, serene and wise,
Guiding us beyond the skies.
With every sigh, we shed our ties,
In this moment, spirit flies.

The weight of worries starts to fade,
In surrender, love is made.
Each breath a prayer, a silent plea,
In the whisper, we are free.

The world spins on, a sacred dance,
In the stillness, we take our chance.
With open hearts, we let it flow,
In letting be, we come to know.

Shedding the Burden of Self

In the mirror, shadows lie,
Reflections of our broken ties.
Yet in the depths, a light appears,
Guiding us beyond our fears.

Letting go of the heavy stone,
We discover we're not alone.
In grace, we rise, and still we fall,
Love's embrace, the greatest call.

With every tear, the layers peel,
Unraveling the heart to heal.
In the silence, wisdom speaks,
Finding strength in softest peaks.

The journey flows like a sacred stream,
In shedding self, we find the beam.
Connection blooms, a divine thread,
In unity, our spirits spread.

The Radiance of Release

From chains of doubt, we break away,
In the dawn of a brand new day.
Releasing burdens, we learn to soar,
In openness, we find the core.

The heart expands, embracing light,
In vulnerability, we ignite.
Each moment holds a sacred choice,
In trust, we find our steady voice.

As petals fall from the weary tree,
In the dance of life, we learn to be.
The vibrant hues of hope arise,
In release, we touch the skies.

Whispers of love fill the air,
In every breath, a tender prayer.
The radiance within, now awake,
In this freedom, our hearts take.

The Calm After the Storm

When thunder fades, and peace aligns,
The spirit whispers in soft designs.
Through chaos, we find our way,
In quiet moments, love will play.

The clouds disperse, revealing grace,
In the stillness, we find our place.
Every drop sings a lullaby,
As nature breathes a healing sigh.

We gather strength from what remains,
In unity, we share the pains.
With open hearts, we mend the seams,
In the calm, we weave our dreams.

The sun breaks forth, a radiant glow,
In the aftermath, we learn to grow.
With each heartbeat, love will transform,
Bringing warmth in the calm after the storm.

Trusting the Light Beyond Control

In shadows deep, we seek the flame,
A guiding force, a holy name.
Through trials vast, we learn to stand,
With open hearts, we trust the hand.

The path ahead may twist and wind,
Yet in each step, the light we find.
With faith as compass, we abide,
In every challenge, peace provided.

The storms may roar, the night seem long,
Yet in our souls, a silent song.
We walk with strength, though fears may rise,
For in the light, we find the wise.

Through doubts that tether, spirits soar,
In every doubt, He opens doors.
The light reveals what's yet to be,
In trusting Him, we are set free.

Emptiness as Sacred Space

Within the void, a sacred place,
Where silence speaks of His embrace.
In emptiness, our hearts unwind,
The stillness whispers, peace we find.

Let go of burdens, cast aside,
In perfect quiet, spirits bide.
Each fleeting thought, a way to see,
That in the void, we're truly free.

The absence blooms, a space divine,
Where love can dance and light entwine.
In every breath, creation stirs,
In emptiness, the soul prefers.

From barren grounds, the blossoms rise,
With every tear, we reach the skies.
In sacred silence, hearts ignite,
For in the void, we find the light.

The Divine Dance of Yielding

A gentle sway, the heart must yield,
To rhythms pure, the soul is healed.
In every movement, spirit flows,
The dance of grace, the heart knows.

With hands outstretched, we let go fear,
In trust divine, He draws us near.
To give and take, a sacred tune,
In yielding hearts, we find the boon.

The flow of life, a woven thread,
In every turn, the path we tread.
From softest whispers, strength is born,
In yielding, life does not forlorn.

With every turn, the spirit spins,
In surrender, we find what wins.
The divine dance, a holy chance,
To touch the grace in every glance.

Blossoming in Full Abandon

In gardens green, the flowers bloom,
With open hearts, dispelling gloom.
Each petal soft, a story told,
In full abandon, beauty unfolds.

No fear of fall, we rise anew,
In every color, faith shines through.
With sunlight's kiss, we stretch and grow,
In blossoming, true love we show.

The winds may blow, the storms may rage,
Yet in our hearts, we turn the page.
With joy as roots, we stand upright,
In every challenge, we ignite.

For in each moment, freedom sings,
In fullest bloom, our spirit wings.
With courage vast, we face the day,
In full abandon, we find our way.

Embrace the Divine Silence

In the stillness, hear the call,
A whisper echoes, love for all.
Beneath the stars, our hearts align,
In sacred hush, we find the Divine.

Moments pause, the world stands still,
In quietude, we learn God's will.
With every breath, the spirit soars,
Embracing peace that ever pours.

The silence wraps like gentle hands,
A cloak of grace, where faith expands.
In every heartbeat, prayer unfolds,
In the stillness, the truth beholds.

Listen closely, the spirit sings,
In the quiet, eternal springs.
Together here, we find our way,
Embracing silence, night and day.

The Weight of Faith

Across the path, where shadows dwell,
The weight of faith, a sacred spell.
In trials faced, we stand upright,
Carrying hope, our guiding light.

Each burden shared, a step we take,
In love's embrace, no hearts will break.
Through storms and strife, we hold on tight,
In unity, we find the right.

When doubts arise, and fears contrive,
The weight of faith helps us survive.
With every tear, a grace bestowed,
In sacred trust, love's journey flowed.

Roots grow deep, the spirit strong,
Together here, we all belong.
In faith's embrace, we shall not fall,
For love transcends, embracing all.

Lightness in the Spirit

In joy's embrace, the spirit lifts,
A dance of hope, our hearts it gifts.
With every flutter, bliss ignites,
In lightness found, our soul takes flight.

Breathe in the glow, let worries fade,
In laughter shared, our fears are laid.
With open hearts, we greet the dawn,
In lightness of spirit, we are reborn.

In gratitude, we walk the path,
Embracing love, avoiding wrath.
Every moment, a chance to rejoice,
In harmony, we make our choice.

The light within, forever shines,
With radiant grace, our spirit twines.
In unity, we rise and sing,
For depth of joy is everything.

Trusting the Unseen

In the depths of the unknown, we tread,
With trust in the unseen, dreams are fed.
In shadows cast, the light will grow,
Embracing faith in all we sow.

Through tangled paths, our spirits roam,
In every heart, we find a home.
The unseen guides, with gentle hand,
Creating hope in faith's vast land.

No fear shall grasp, nor doubt confine,
In trusting grace, our souls entwine.
Believing in the journey's art,
In every step, we find the heart.

So let us walk with heads held high,
For in the unseen, love's wings do fly.
In trusting whispers, the truth we glean,
Embracing all that lies between.

Floating on Faith's Breath

In the stillness, hearts arise,
Lifted by wings, beyond the skies.
Whispers of hope in gentle streams,
Carrying forth our deepest dreams.

The light cascades on hands outstretched,
Each pulse of grace, our souls are etched.
Guided by love, we soar and sway,
Floating on faith, we find our way.

In shadows cast, yet not alone,
Divine assurance, our sacred tone.
Castles of doubt may fall away,
As we trust in night, as well as day.

Through storms that rage and winds that howl,
In quiet moments, we hear the vow.
Holding the truth, forever near,
Floating on faith, we conquer fear.

With every breath, a prayer takes flight,
Cradled in peace, we embrace the light.
Journeying forth, hearts intertwined,
Floating on faith, forever aligned.

In the Arms of Infinite Possibility

In the silence of a new dawn,
Hope awakens, fears are gone.
Every moment, a choice to make,
In faith's embrace, our spirits awake.

Boundless paths lie before our eyes,
Embracing truths in vast skies.
Infinite dreams await to unfold,
In possibilities, we are bold.

With tender hands, we weave our prayer,
A tapestry rich, woven with care.
Each stitch a promise, love's decree,
In the arms of grace, we are free.

Through valleys low and mountains high,
In unity, our souls will fly.
With every step towards the light,
In the arms of hope, we find our sight.

Let go of limits, let faith expand,
In every heartbeat, a chance at hand.
Together we'll rise, we'll soar, we'll be,
In the arms of infinite possibility.

The Courage to Unclasp

In shadows cursed, where silence dwells,
A whisper stirs, the spirit swells.
To lift the veil, to break the chain,
The courage blooms amidst the pain.

In troubled waters, faith takes hold,
Unraveling fears, like threads of gold.
Each step unbound, we find release,
The courage to unclasp, to seek peace.

With every heartbeat, strength is born,
In the darkest nights, the light is worn.
Through trials faced and lessons learned,
The courage kindles, brightly burned.

To soar beyond the cage we've made,
Through love's soft touch, all doubt will fade.
With open hearts, we embrace the call,
The courage to unclasp, to rise for all.

As spirits dance, no longer confined,
In love's sweet embrace, our souls entwined.
With every breath, we dare to trust,
The courage to unclasp, in faith we must.

A Leap Toward the Eternal

With trembling hearts, we stand on grace,
A leap of faith, we choose our place.
The edge of dreams, where courage lies,
A leap toward truth, beyond the skies.

In faith we find, the strength to leap,
Into the arms of love so deep.
Boundless horizons, a future bright,
A leap toward hope, embracing light.

Let doubts disperse, like shadows fade,
In sacred moments, the path is laid.
With open hearts, we make our vow,
A leap toward life, we take it now.

As spirits soar on wings of trust,
United with the Divine, we must.
Through every challenge, we will ignite,
A leap toward joy, our souls take flight.

For in the leap, we find the way,
Releasing burdens, we will sway.
Together we dance, a divine swirl,
A leap toward the eternal, we unfurl.

Tranquil Liberation

In silence deep, the spirit stirs,
A tranquil heart, where hope concurs.
Beneath the skies, a soft embrace,
In faith we find our sacred space.

Through whispered prayers, the dawn unfolds,
A gentle touch, the truth it holds.
In every breath, we rise anew,
To liberate the soul so true.

The rivers flow, they cleanse the night,
With each new wave, they bring the light.
Through trials faced, we learn to soar,
In harmony, we seek the shore.

A stillness found within the storm,
In every shadow, love's light warm.
We dance in grace, our spirits blend,
In tranquil peace, our hearts ascend.

The world may tremble, yet we stand,
With open hearts, and lifted hands.
To be released, to be made whole,
In tranquil liberation, find your soul.

The Pathway to Peace

Upon the road where calm does lie,
We seek the truth, beneath the sky.
With every step, a chance anew,
In sacred silence, we find what's true.

The pathway calls, with gentle grace,
A journey shared, our love's embrace.
With faith as guide, we walk in light,
Each moment brings a deeper sight.

Beneath the stars, our spirits rise,
In every tear, a cherished prize.
Through valleys low and mountains high,
In peace we find our wings to fly.

The whispers soft, they lead us near,
To trust the heart, to quell the fear.
In unity, our voices blend,
On the pathway, hearts transcend.

From shadows past, we step away,
In every dawn, a brighter day.
With love as beacon, souls release,
Together on this path of peace.

The Sacred Unfurling

In morning light, the petals bloom,
A sacred dance dispels the gloom.
With each soft sigh, the spirit wakes,
In silence pure, the heart partakes.

Through every breath, the essence flows,
In stillness deep, the spirit knows.
As leaves unfurl, we find our way,
In sacred trust, the light will stay.

The stars above, in whispers share,
The secrets held in love's true care.
Through sacred time, our journey's cast,
In every moment, truth holds fast.

With hands extended, hearts align,
To feel the grace, in love's design.
In harmony, the soul may sing,
In sacred unfurling, freedom brings.

In twilight's glow, we seek the dawn,
Creating space for love to spawn.
With open hearts, we rise above,
In sacred unfurling, we find love.

Love's Unchained Whispers

In gentle breeze, love's whispers call,
A tender glance, where shadows fall.
With every word, we break the chain,
In unison, we dance through pain.

The stars align, our spirits blend,
In love's embrace, we find the mend.
Through trials faced, our hearts ignite,
In unchained whispers, we're in flight.

The moonlight guides, a silver thread,
With every sigh, the past is shed.
In unity, our hearts arise,
In love's pure light, no need for guise.

With open arms, we share the grace,
In every smile, a soft embrace.
Through love we find, our souls take wing,
In unchained whispers, hearts will sing.

As dawn awakes, we greet the day,
With love unchained, we find our way.
In every heartbeat, truth prevails,
In love's sweet whispers, life unveils.

Echoes of the Divine

In silence, a whisper sings,
God's love in the simple things.
A light that dances in our heart,
Reminding us we are each a part.

With faith we walk the narrow way,
Through shadows that bend and sway.
Each prayer a star in the sky,
Guiding souls as they reply.

From mountains high to valleys low,
Divine warmth in every glow.
In the stillness, hope refrains,
In the storm, eternal gains.

The sacred breath that lifts us near,
In every sigh, we find Him here.
His essence flows through all we see,
In every leaf, in every tree.

To hear the echoes of the light,
Through every day, through every night.
In unity, we raise our song,
In harmony, where we belong.

The Old and the New

In ancient ways, the truth unfolds,
In stories whispered, life beholds.
Wisdom ages like fine wine,
Transforms the heart, the soul divine.

Old scriptures guide, a steadfast hand,
In changing tides, we understand.
With each new dawn, the promise grows,
The seeds of faith, like rivers, flow.

Traditions blend, a vibrant loom,
Weaving paths from the past's womb.
In every ritual, love ignites,
Binding hearts, soaring to heights.

The old and new in sacred dance,
A timeless bond, a holy chance.
In every moment, grace reborn,
Through loss and hope, we are adorned.

Together we rise, embrace the light,
In faith, we journey day and night.
In harmony, we find our way,
The past and present, come what may.

Elysian Letting

In the stillness of a quiet morn,
We let go of burdens worn.
With open hearts, we breathe in peace,
In this moment, all troubles cease.

Each tear, a blessing from above,
Washing us clean in gentle love.
With every sigh, we cast away,
The shadows that led us astray.

In surrender, we learn to trust,
In every grain of sacred dust.
We release the weight of yesterday,
Finding joy in the present's sway.

The spirit dances, light and free,
In the letting go, we truly see.
With open hands and open hearts,
A new beginning artfully starts.

From chaos blooms a garden fair,
In the letting, we feel His care.
In every ending, a new way flows,
In Elysian letting, love bestows.

A Journey Beyond This Realm

We wander paths unseen and bright,
With faith to guide us through the night.
Beyond the stars, our spirits soar,
In realms where love forever pours.

Each heartbeat echoes what is true,
A promise born, a covenant new.
With trust, we cross dimensions wide,
In grace, our souls no longer hide.

The veil grows thin, as whispers call,
In every rise, in every fall.
The light of Heaven warms our skin,
Inviting us to journey in.

As shadows fade, the dawn shall break,
In every breath, a path we take.
Through trials faced, our spirits rise,
For in the end, love never dies.

A tapestry of life we weave,
In faith and hope, we shall believe.
Together we roam, hand in hand,
Beyond this realm, where we shall stand.

The Quietude of Faith

In stillness, whispers rise,
Heaven's touch, soft as a sigh.
Hearts entwined in sacred grace,
Seeking truth in quiet space.

Beneath the stars, we find our way,
A path of light, come what may.
In gentle breath, we trust the night,
Faith's embrace, our guiding light.

Through trials, storms, and endless doubt,
The soul's refrain will cry out loud.
With fervor strong, we stand as one,
In faith, our battles bravely won.

Harmony in sacred prayer,
Angels heed our heartfelt care.
Each moment blessed, a gift divine,
In quietude, our spirits shine.

Let doubts dissolve like morning dew,
In faith's embrace, we're born anew.
With humble hearts, we raise our song,
To the quietude where we belong.

Seraphic Letting Loose

Wings unfurl in joyful flight,
Celestial dance in the light.
Hearts ablaze with love's embrace,
Seraphic whispers fill the space.

Free our souls, let spirits soar,
In sacred revelry, we implore.
Find the joy in every breath,
Celebrating life and conquering death.

In laughter's song, the heavens sing,
As boundless grace takes to the wing.
Together, let our voices blend,
A symphony that knows no end.

With every step, our faith expands,
We dance with joy, hand in hand.
The world transformed, a vibrant hue,
In seraphic light, we are made new.

Let worries fade in love's embrace,
Find our strength in sacred space.
With spirits high, in unity,
We let loose in seraphic glee.

In the Hands of the Divine

Cradled gently, we are blessed,
In the palms of love, we rest.
Every heartbeat, every prayer,
In the hands that always care.

When shadows fall and doubts arise,
We look up to the endless skies.
With faith ignited, spirits climb,
In the hands of the divine.

Broken pieces, healed with grace,
Through trials, we find our place.
Surrendered hearts, so free and pure,
In the hands of love, we endure.

Moments fleeting, time will fade,
Yet in His hand, we are remade.
Hope unfurls, a sacred vine,
Rooted deep in the divine.

Each dawn a promise, ever bright,
Guided forth by endless light.
Together we rise, come what may,
In the hands of the divine, we stay.

Dawn of Resurgence

When darkness fades, the light does break,
A new beginning, hearts awake.
In the twilight, spirits rise,
Embracing hope beneath the skies.

Each shadow past, a lesson learned,
In the fire of grace, we've burned.
From ashes, life begins anew,
In every heart, the spark shines through.

With every breath, we breathe in strength,
In unity, we go the length.
Awakening, our spirits sing,
Dawn of resurgence, love's offering.

No more chains to hold us fast,
We rise with courage, free at last.
Through trials faced, we find our way,
The dawn of hope begins to sway.

Together, side by side we stand,
In faith's embrace, we feel His hand.
A brighter world, a love that's true,
Dawn of resurgence, born anew.

The Mystic's Atonement

In shadows cast by light divine,
I seek the path, a sacred sign.
With whispers soft, the soul's embrace,
I gather grace in quiet space.

Each tear a prayer, each sigh a vow,
To cleanse the heart, to humble now.
In stillness found, the truth I glean,
The weight of worlds, a fleeting dream.

Through trials faced, I rise anew,
Transcending pain with love so true.
The sacred flame within me glows,
In darkened nights, my spirit flows.

I walk the earth, yet soar above,
In every struggle, I find love.
The mystic's heart, my guiding star,
In silence deep, I'm never far.

In every moment, a song unfolds,
Of ancient tales that time beholds.
The atonement found in every breath,
A dance of life, defying death.

Fruits of Surrender

In fields of faith, where dreams abide,
The fruits of love, they bloom inside.
With tender hands, I plant the seeds,
Of grace and hope, of gentle deeds.

In letting go, the heart takes flight,
Embracing all, both dark and light.
The harvest comes, rich and profound,
In quiet moments, joy is found.

With humble spirit, I trust the way,
Each step a prayer, a sacred play.
The sun may set, but dawn will break,
In surrender's grace, my soul awakes.

The journey's course, both long and wide,
Leads me to peace, my faithful guide.
With gratitude, I walk the lane,
In every loss, a glimpse of gain.

The fruits of surrender, sweet and rare,
In every breath, a whispered prayer.
I hold them close, these gifts bestowed,
In love's embrace, I'm gently sowed.

The Child's Innocent Trust

A child's heart, so pure and free,
In wonder's gaze, the joy to see.
With spirits bright, they roam the land,
In every moment, grace at hand.

Each laugh a melody, soft and clear,
In every whisper, faith draws near.
The world unfolds, a tale untold,
In innocent trust, their love behold.

They reach for stars, the skies above,
With open hearts, they share their love.
In simple faith, they walk the line,
With hands held high, their spirits shine.

The beauty found in every glance,
A dance of hope, a sacred chance.
The child within, we must embrace,
To find our way, to seek His grace.

In days of doubt, let us return,
To childlike trust, our hearts must yearn.
In every heartbeat, life anew,
The child's dream, forever true.

Wings that Fly Beyond

With wings outspread, I long to soar,
Above the clouds, to wisdom's shore.
In every heartbeat, strength I find,
To break the chains that keep me blind.

Through trials faced, my spirit learns,
In every light, a flame that burns.
The winds of change, they lift me high,
In faith's embrace, I learn to fly.

I chase the stars, the moonlit sky,
With open arms, I dare to try.
In freedom's dance, my soul expands,
A journey led by unseen hands.

Through valleys deep and mountains tall,
In every heartbeat, I heed the call.
With wings of grace, I find my place,
In love's compassion, I touch His face.

Beyond the veil, where visions gleam,
In every breath, I dare to dream.
The wings that fly, they guide my way,
In sacred trust, I choose to stay.

Unbinding the Heart

In shadows deep, the spirit cries,
Yearning for light beneath the skies.
Chains of sorrow slowly break,
Love's embrace begins to wake.

In prayerful whispers, echoes sound,
The heart unbound, no more confound.
With faith as guide, no fear, no plight,
The dawn reveals a new-found light.

Each tear a gift, each hope a song,
In trust, we learn where we belong.
A tapestry of grace unfolds,
In warmth of love, our truth beholds.

The light within begins to blaze,
Illuminating all our ways.
With open arms, we now embrace,
The wondrous gift of love and grace.

With every breath, the heart will rise,
Reaching for love that never dies.
In freeing vows, our souls take flight,
In unity, we find the light.

Finding Freedom in Faith

In stillness found within the heart,
We seek the truth, a brand-new start.
With every prayer, a bond we weave,
In faith's embrace, we learn to believe.

Through valleys low, and mountains high,
We lift our hands, we touch the sky.
In every struggle, grace appears,
In faith, we conquer all our fears.

A quiet strength in souls who long,
To share the light, to lift the song.
As branches bend but do not break,
In faith we find what hope can make.

Each step we take, the path grows clear,
In love, in trust, we persevere.
With every heartbeat, spirit sings,
In freedom found, our spirit wings.

Together bound, we rise and soar,
In faith, our hearts forever more.
With open eyes, we see the grace,
In every moment, every place.

The Quiet Offering of Surrender

In silence sweet, we drop our guard,
In whispered prayers, we lift the hard.
With open hands, we let go strife,
In surrender, we find new life.

The burdens fall, like autumn leaves,
In quiet trust, the spirit cleaves.
With gentle hearts, we turn to Thee,
In surrender's grace, we learn to be.

In every trial, a lesson learned,
In every fall, our souls have turned.
We rise anew, as dawn bestows,
The beauty found when faith just grows.

In softest whispers, peace will reign,
In letting go, we lose the pain.
The quiet offering humbly shared,
A life transformed, a heart laid bare.

With every breath, a chance to see,
The sacred bond, in you and me.
In trust and love, we find our way,
Surrendered hearts, our souls at play.

Wings of Grace Breaking Free

Upon the winds, our spirits rise,
With wings of grace that touch the skies.
In every heartbeat, echoes soar,
A sacred dance, forevermore.

In trials faced, we find our strength,
In love, we travel any length.
With open hearts, we seek the truth,
In every moment, love's sweet youth.

The chains that bind begin to break,
With every step, we dare to take.
In faith's embrace, we come alive,
With wings of grace, we learn to thrive.

A tapestry woven in the light,
With every choice, we turn the night.
In guiding stars, our paths unite,
In love's pure warmth, we find our flight.

So let us rise, and freely sing,
In faith's embrace, our spirits bring.
With wings of grace, the sky's our home,
In unity, we cease to roam.

The Spirit's Journey Home

Through valleys deep, the spirit roams,
In search of light, it longs for homes.
With wings of grace, and heart of fire,
It seeks the place of pure desire.

In whispered prayers, the echoes call,
A distant shore where shadows fall.
Each star a guide, each wave a song,
To where the soul has known its throng.

The winding path, though steep and wide,
Shows glimpses of the truth inside.
With every step, the spirit learns,
A dance of trust, as quiet yearns.

In twilight's glow, the dance unfolds,
A journey rich with tales retold.
With every sigh, the heart ascends,
To find the peace that never ends.

Now home at last, the spirit sighs,
In sacred light, it softly lies.
The journey long, yet worth the roam,
As love embraces, spirit's home.

Sacred Whispers of Departure

In quietude, the soul prepares,
For sacred whispers, love declares.
With hearts entwined, we say goodbye,
To realms beyond, we gently fly.

Each moment shared, a cherished flame,
Guiding spirits, none are the same.
In love's embrace, we find our peace,
As earthly ties begin to cease.

The breath of life, a sacred song,
Carries us where we belong.
With open hearts, we take our flight,
Into the vast, embracing light.

Through veils of time, we weave our fate,
With every step, we contemplate.
The blessings come, as shadows fade,
In trust, we walk, unafraid.

In whispered winds, our hearts unite,
In every dawn, the spirit's light.
A journey forth, into the grace,
Of love eternal, our sacred space.

The Dance of Surrender

In twilight hues, the spirit bends,
To love's embrace, where journey ends.
With open arms, we let it flow,
In dance of grace, we learn to know.

Through trials faced, in shadows deep,
The call of faith, the love we keep.
Surrendered hearts, we softly share,
As each step takes us further there.

In circles spun, our souls align,
With every heartbeat, gently twine.
A symphony of trust and light,
Embracing all, as day turns night.

In stillness found, the whispers bloom,
In letting go, we lose the gloom.
The dance eternal, woven tight,
In every breath, the purest sight.

So here we stand, in open flow,
With every step, we come to know.
The dance of life, a sacred prayer,
In surrender's grace, we're always there.

The Blessing of Easing

In gentle hands, we find release,
A tender grace, a moment's peace.
As burdens lift, the spirit soars,
In quiet stillness, love restores.

The heart unwinds, a soft refrain,
As whispered blessings wash the pain.
In nature's arms, we learn to breathe,
And in surrender, joys believe.

Each step we take, a mindful pause,
In every breath, the spirit draws.
A sacred trust in what will be,
In opening hearts, we find the key.

With open eyes, we see the light,
A journey wound in day and night.
The blessing comes, as we release,
In ebb and flow, the heart's increase.

So let us dwell in easing's grace,
In love's embrace, we find our place.
In every moment, life bestowed,
A blessing deep, our hearts' abode.

Forsaken Fears

In shadows deep, the heart does quake,
Yet faith can heal the soul's mistake.
With whispered prayers, our doubts will cease,
In grace we find our perfect peace.

The storm may rage, the night be long,
But in His arms, we find our song.
Forsaken fears, we cast away,
For love divine will guide our way.

Upon the path where hope is sown,
We journey forth, not all alone.
The light will break, the dawn will shine,
In sacred trust, His hand is mine.

So let us rise from depths of night,
In every shadow, find the light.
Our hearts unbound, we learn to soar,
In faith, we find forevermore.

With every step, the spirit's flight,
We leave behind the chains of fright.
In holy whispers, fears will fade,
By faith restored, our souls remade.

The Unfolding of Trust

In quiet moments, trust begins,
A gentle seed that growth brings in.
With open hearts, we brave the dawn,
In every trial, our fears are gone.

Unfolding petals, grace's flow,
A sacred dance where spirits glow.
With every breath, we learn to see,
In trust, we find our destiny.

The tapestry of life is spun,
Each thread a story, each heart a sun.
With faith as anchor, we stand strong,
Together, where we all belong.

When shadows whisper, doubt takes flight,
We hold to truth, our guiding light.
In love's embrace, we learn to share,
The warmth of trust, forever rare.

So let us walk this path divine,
In every moment, thy will be mine.
The unfolding trust, a sacred bind,
In spirit bound, our souls aligned.

Chasing the Celestial

With eyes uplifted to the sky,
We chase the stars that never die.
In every twinkle, dreams ignite,
Their brilliance guides us through the night.

The heavens sing a timeless tune,
A melody that whispers soon.
With each step taken on this earth,
We find our purpose, we find our worth.

In cosmic dance, the truth unfolds,
A story woven with threads of gold.
We chase the light, embracing grace,
In every moment, we find our place.

Through trials faced, we rise anew,
With every heartbeat, love shines through.
In celestial arms, we learn to fly,
Together bound, you and I.

So let us journey, hand in hand,
In faith we soar, forever stand.
Chasing the celestial, our hearts ablaze,
In endless wonder, we spend our days.

Prayerful Release

In whispered prayers, we find our peace,
A gentle letting go, sweet release.
With open hearts, we seek His grace,
In every moment, love's embrace.

The burdens lifted, spirits free,
In faith we trust, and we will see.
With every tear, a healing flow,
In prayerful whispers, hearts will glow.

Release the weight that burdens our soul,
In sacred trust, we are made whole.
Let go of fears that blind the sight,
In prayerful peace, we find our light.

As seasons change, the spirit rises,
In every moment, new surprises.
From shadows past, we turn and face,
In love's sweet grace, we leave this space.

So gather now, let praises soar,
In unified hearts, we seek for more.
With prayerful release, our souls take flight,
Together bound in love's pure light.

Whispers from Heaven

In silence, Divine words call,
A gentle breeze lifts our souls,
Guiding us through the shadows,
To the light where love enrolls.

Angels' laughter fills the air,
With each prayer, a soul ascends,
Hope rekindles in our hearts,
As the path of faith extends.

Hearts unite in sacred song,
In harmony, we find our way,
Through trials, we grow strong,
In trust, we seek the day.

With every tear, a blessing shines,
In every sorrow, joy will bloom,
A tapestry woven by the Divine,
In grace, there is no gloom.

Together we walk, hand in hand,
Following whispers from above,
A journey of faith, forever grand,
Wrapped in the warmth of love.

Blessed Departure

As dusk settles on weary eyes,
The call to rest is softly spoken,
A journey awaits beyond the skies,
In peace, no heart is broken.

With every step, the spirit soars,
Released from earthly chains that bind,
Embraced by love that ever pours,
A new beginning, truth shall find.

Farewell to tears and earthly strife,
In His arms, we find our place,
In the embrace of eternal life,
We breathe in solace, filled with grace.

Though shadows fall upon the ground,
The light above forever shines,
In the silence, love is found,
A journey, divine, that intertwines.

With gratitude, we rise and go,
Into the arms of endless light,
A blessed departure, a soft glow,
In faith, we take our flight.

The Trust of a Pilgrim's Heart

In the stillness, a heart does beat,
A wanderer searching for the way,
With each step, a sacred feat,
Faith whispers, 'Trust in the day.'

Mountains may rise, storms may roar,
Yet in the depths of the heart,
A fire burns, a steadfast core,
Guiding the soul, a sacred art.

With every trial, a lesson learned,
In the valley, hope ignites,
A pilgrim's journey, brightly turned,
Faith's lantern glowing through the nights.

The promise of dawn calls us near,
We lay our burdens down with grace,
In the quiet, the Divine draws near,
Together, we seek His embrace.

Though the path may twist and bend,
Each step taken, a prayer unspun,
Trusting in love that knows no end,
A pilgrimage where we are one.

Sacred Journey to Freedom

On sacred paths where spirits roam,
We tread the earth with humble pride,
Each step a whisper, a call back home,
In faith, we cease to hide.

Chains of doubt fall to the ground,
As truth illuminates the way,
In every heart, freedom is found,
Awakening to a brighter day.

The song of hope entwines our souls,
With every breath, we rise anew,
In unity, the Spirit consoles,
Drawing us closer to what is true.

Through valleys deep and mountains high,
Love leads us forth without retreat,
Our journey vast, beneath the sky,
In freedom's grace, our hearts will beat.

Step by step, let courage rise,
In each heart, a flame ignites,
A sacred journey, reaching for the skies,
Together, we embrace the light.

Release of the Soul's Grasp

In shadows deep where spirits dwell,
The heart cries out, a sacred spell.
To break the chains, I seek the light,
In whispers soft, the dawn takes flight.

With every tear, a burden fades,
The soul ascends through faith's cascades.
Hand in hand with grace I rise,
To touch the sky, to hear the cries.

The weight of fears, a fading ghost,
In gentle winds, I find my post.
Beyond the veil, a promise glows,
In holy trust, my spirit knows.

Release me, Lord, from earthly ties,
In sacred breath, my spirit flies.
Through trials met and lessons earned,
In divine love, my soul returned.

At journey's end, in blissful peace,
In Your embrace, my fears release.
For every step was meant to be,
In Your embrace, I am set free.

The Sacred Surrender

In quiet moments, the heart finds rest,
A whisper sweet, of love confess'd.
To lay my burdens at Your feet,
In sacred trust, my soul's retreat.

The world around, so loud, so near,
Yet in Your arms, I conquer fear.
All paths were forged by hands divine,
In every trial, Your light will shine.

With every breath, a prayer takes flight,
In every shadow, You are the light.
Surrendered now, my spirit sings,
In sacred peace, my heart takes wing.

Through storms that rage and nights so long,
In trusting hearts, we find our song.
Each wave a lesson, each tear a chance,
In holy grace, our spirits dance.

In surrender's grace, I rise anew,
With faith as guide, I walk with You.
For in each moment, love prevails,
In sacred surrender, my spirit sails.

In the Embrace of Divine Release

O gentle Spirit, draw me near,
In sacred silence, calm my fear.
Through trials faced and tears I've shed,
In Your embrace, my soul is fed.

Release me from the chains I bear,
In Your sweet light, I find my prayer.
A trust so deep, it lifts me high,
In boundless love, I learn to fly.

Each moment spent in faith's own light,
Leads me away from darkest night.
Your mercies flow, like rivers wide,
In every heartache, You abide.

With every breath, I feel Your grace,
In sacred moments, I find my place.
In silent whispers, the truth unfolds,
In Your embrace, my spirit molds.

In joyful thanks, I now receive,
The love that allows my heart to breathe.
For in Your hands, my fears release,
In divine warmth, I find my peace.

Threads of Faith Unraveled

In tapestry of light and dark,
Each thread a story, each thread a spark.
Woven tight, yet pulled apart,
In faithful hands, we find each heart.

As shadows fall, and doubts arise,
In faith we trust, and wisdom ties.
With every fear, the thread grows thin,
Yet woven strong, I begin again.

The loom of life spins tales untold,
In vibrant hues, both young and old.
Through trials faced, the fabric weaves,
In love's embrace, the spirit believes.

As years unfold, and paths diverge,
Each step I take, to You I urge.
The threads of faith, though frayed they seem,
Are woven whole, in love's sweet dream.

And at the end, when all is bare,
I'll stand renewed, in love laid bare.
Each thread a testament we weave,
In faith and grace, we learn to believe.

Serene Grace Released

In whispers soft, the spirit flows,
A gentle tide where stillness grows.
In quiet trust, the heart will lie,
Beneath the watchful, endless sky.

With every breath, the burdens fade,
In sacred light, all fears arrayed.
The soul takes flight on wings of peace,
In grace, our troubles find release.

The world may thunder, clash, and weep,
Yet in the stillness, love runs deep.
We find our strength in silent prayer,
And know that we are met with care.

In humble awe, we seek the way,
To walk in light, to bless the day.
For in our hearts, the truth remains,
In every joy, in every pain.

So let us rise with tranquil heart,
In unity, we'll not depart.
Together bound, we share this grace,
In every step, a sacred space.

Heavenly Abandon

In open arms, the heavens call,
To those who stumble, rise, and fall.
With faith as winds beneath our wings,
We dance to love, as freedom sings.

The stars above, they shine so bright,
A map for souls who seek the light.
With every step, the path we tread,
Guided by promises long said.

Let go the weight of earthly chains,
In pure surrender, joy remains.
The heart, aflame, ignites the night,
In every tear, a spark of light.

As echoes fade, the silence speaks,
In stillness found, the spirit seeks.
The sacred whispers in our ears,
Transform our doubts, dissolve our fears.

With eyes of faith, behold the dawn,
A canvas bright for us to spawn.
Together here, we leap and soar,
In heavenly abandon, evermore.

In the Reverence of Release

In quietude, our spirits rise,
Like morning mist that meets the skies.
With gentle hands and grateful hearts,
We set aside our heavy parts.

In reverence, we learn to yield,
The harvest found upon the field.
With every sigh, we breathe anew,
In letting go, our strength comes through.

Lifted high, the chains dissolve,
In unity, our souls evolve.
The ancient songs within us swell,
In harmony, all is made well.

We walk a path of sacred trust,
In faith we rise, in love we must.
Beyond the hurt, beyond the fray,
In tender mercy, light holds sway.

So, cast away what holds you fast,
Embrace the future, learn from the past.
And in the reverence of release,
We find our hearts, we shape our peace.

The Lantern of Liberation

In darkened nights, a lantern glows,
Its light a guide where wisdom flows.
With every step, we shed the night,
And walk together towards the light.

The flame within can never die,
As love ignites, we cannot lie.
Through trials faced, our spirits shine,
In liberation, all is divine.

With open hearts, we share our song,
In unity, we all belong.
The trials past, they shape our grace,
In every joy, we find our place.

The lantern draws us ever near,
A sacred bond that casts out fear.
With every dawn, we rise anew,
In peace we walk, in love we strew.

So trust the light, let hope unfurl,
In the lantern's glow, we change the world.
Together bound by love's decree,
In liberation, we are free.

In the Presence of the Divine

In whispers soft, the Spirit calls,
We gather near, beneath the thralls.
In sacred time, our hearts unite,
In the glow of love, pure and bright.

Amidst the peace, we find our aim,
To honor Him, to bless His name.
In humble prayer, our voices soar,
In every breath, we seek Him more.

A light descends, it warms the heart,
In each embrace, we play our part.
An endless grace, where souls align,
In the presence of the Divine.

We seek the truth, our spirits free,
In every leaf, in every tree.
The beauty here, it speaks of love,
A gift bestowed from arms above.

With every step, we walk the way,
Through shadows deep, we rise and pray.
In faithful hearts, His love is found,
In blissful joy, our souls abound.

Faithful Farewells

In quiet hours, we share our pain,
With tearful eyes, we gather, pray.
Each whispered word, a tender balm,
In faith we trust, the heart stays calm.

Though parting comes, we hold the grace,
In memories dear, we find our place.
With spirits bound, our love remains,
In shadows cast, no one complains.

A journey ends, yet life persists,
In every hug, a gentle kiss.
The bonds we forged, forever tight,
In heart and mind, they gleam so bright.

The skies may weep for those we miss,
Yet in our hearts, there's hope and bliss.
For every end, a new hello,
In faith, we trust, the love will grow.

So take these words, like stars above,
In sacred light, we find our love.
In faithful farewells, we rejoice,
In every prayer, we hear His voice.

Spirit's Lightness

In gentle winds, the Spirit flows,
With every breath, a promise grows.
In dawning light, our spirits rise,
In sacred love, we touch the skies.

Each vibrant hue, a song of grace,
In harmony, we find our place.
With open hearts, we learn to soar,
In lightness found, we seek no more.

A dance of joy, with grace we tread,
In every note, our souls are fed.
With lifted hands, we praise and sing,
In every moment, the Spirit's wing.

From shadows past, we step into light,
In faith we walk, with hearts so bright.
For in our soul, the truth is clear,
In Spirit's lightness, we find cheer.

So let us rise, with courage bold,
In every life, His love unfold.
With hearts aglow, we walk the way,
In Spirit's light, we greet each day.

Seraphic Release

In heavenly realms, the angels sing,
With wings of love, their praises ring.
In purest light, our souls take flight,
In seraphic grace, we find the right.

The burdens cast into the night,
In whispered prayers, we seek the light.
Through trials faced, our spirits free,
In love's embrace, we find the key.

A gentle touch, from hand to hand,
In unity, together we stand.
The veil is thin, our hearts aglow,
In seraphic release, we grow.

From grief to joy, the journey bends,
With every step, the heart transcends.
In greater love, we find our peace,
In sacred moments, we find release.

So let us dance in harmony,
In every note, a symphony.
With open hearts, we rise above,
In seraphic release, there's only love.

The Gentle Letting Luminous

In the silence of the night, we find,
A whisper soft, a heart unconfined.
Light breaking through the shadows of gloom,
In gentle letting, we begin to bloom.

Casting burdens to the distant sea,
Trusting in the love that sets us free.
Radiant warmth within our soul ignites,
Guiding us into the sacred heights.

With every breath, a prayer takes flight,
In the stillness, we embrace the light.
Luminous grace, our spirits entwined,
In letting go, the truth we find.

Casting doubts like leaves in the stream,
Flowing freely, woven in the dream.
With open hearts, we dance in the glow,
The gentle letting teaches us to grow.

So bask in the warmth, let worries cease,
In the gentle letting, we find our peace.
To live in love, with mercy and trust,
In luminous letting, we rise from dust.

Heart's Awakening

In the stillness, the heart begins to wake,
Whispers of love in every step we take.
With each heartbeat, a sacred song sings,
A melody of hope that peace brings.

From shadows deep, we rise to embrace,
The light of mercy, the warmth of grace.
In forgiving arms, we find our way,
A dawn of joy, a brand new day.

The burdens lifted, our spirits soar,
Each moment a gift, forevermore.
In the quiet hush, a spark ignites,
A heart awakened in divine lights.

Through trials faced, the soul refines,
In every challenge, wisdom aligns.
In Unity's love, we seek and find,
A heart's awakening, pure and kind.

So let the spirit shine and be bold,
In the embrace of love, we break the mold.
With every beat, let faith ascend,
In our hearts, the journey will mend.

The Freedom of Forgiveness

In shadows cast by hurt and by pain,
Forgiveness blooms like a gentle rain.
Washing wounds with compassion's flow,
In the heart's release, our spirits grow.

Chains that bind begin to fall away,
In the light of mercy, we learn to sway.
With courage found, we open the door,
To freedom's path, forevermore.

No longer shackled by the past's embrace,
In forgiveness, we discover grace.
The heart unburdened, it learns to sing,
In the joy of letting go, life takes wing.

Every step on this journey brings peace,
A tapestry woven, our sorrows cease.
In the sacred act of love bestowed,
The freedom of forgiveness is bestowed.

So gather strength, and softly let go,
In the garden of grace, new seeds we sow.
With open arms, we share and mend,
In the freedom of forgiveness, we transcend.

On the Wings of Grace

Beneath the arching heavens, we rise,
On wings of grace, our spirits touch the skies.
With every heartbeat, love's promise unfurls,
In the dance of eternity, our soul whirls.

Through valleys low and mountains high,
In grace's embrace, we learn to fly.
With gentle whispers that guide our way,
We find our strength in the light of day.

In unity's bond, we discover the truth,
The heart of the child, the dreams of youth.
With each connection, a thread we weave,
On the wings of grace, together we believe.

Let go of worries, let burdens fall,
With every leap, we answer the call.
In faith's warm hold, we rise and soar,
On the wings of grace, forevermore.

So lift your eyes, and trust the way,
In the light of grace, we choose to stay.
With open hearts and spirits bright,
On the wings of grace, we embrace the light.

Trusting the Infinite

In silence deep, I hear the call,
A whisper smooth, like morning's thrall.
Beyond the veils, beyond the night,
I find my peace in sacred light.

With every breath, I let doubts cease,
In faith I walk, I find my peace.
Trusting Him who sees my way,
Guiding me through night and day.

His love like rivers flows so free,
A promise binding you and me.
In His embrace, I feel the whole,
Infinite grace that heals my soul.

Through storms I tread, through trials faced,
In every tear, His love is placed.
I rise with wings of hope and grace,
Trusting the Infinite's embrace.

And when the shadows draw me near,
I hold on tight, dispelling fear.
For in the depths, His light will shine,
Trusting the love that's truly divine.

The Alchemy of Abandon

In the stillness, I release my fears,
Embracing light, dissolving tears.
The world fades soft, like morning mist,
In this surrender, I find bliss.

With open hands, I let it go,
Trusting the path, I've yet to know.
The alchemy of faith I taste,
Transformed in love, no moment waste.

In shadows deep, the light will gleam,
Awakened now, I chase the dream.
With every heartbeat, I am reborn,
In this surrender, hope is sworn.

Letting the stars light up my way,
With grace, I dance, I learn to sway.
In loss, I find a greater gain,
The alchemy of joy through pain.

So here I stand, at Heaven's gate,
In pure abandon, I await.
Transform me, Lord, with each new day,
In love and light, I long to stay.

Ascending Through Surrender

In quiet moments, I find my trust,
Releasing burdens, turning to dust.
Ascending dreams on wings of grace,
In sweet surrender, I find my place.

The mountain calls, the path is steep,
Yet in my heart, Your promises keep.
I rise above the doubts that bind,
In surrender's dance, my soul aligned.

Each step I take, Your hand I feel,
In humble prayer, I start to heal.
Through every trial, Your love remains,
Ascending higher, breaking chains.

The stars above, they light my way,
In surrender's heart, I choose to stay.
For in this journey, I'm never alone,
Together forever, we're truly one.

As the dawn breaks, I feel the change,
In this sweet surrender, life's rearranged.
With every heartbeat, I claim my song,
Ascending through surrender, where I belong.

In the Embrace of Shadows

Within the night, a truth resides,
In silent whispers, where love abides.
The shadows dance, they hold a tale,
Of hope and grace that will prevail.

In darkness deep, my spirit grows,
For in the still, the wisdom flows.
I learn to trust the unseen hand,
Guiding me softly, through this land.

With every fear, I greet the night,
In the embrace of shadows, I find light.
For every moment carries grace,
A sacred space, I now embrace.

As stars emerge, their glow ignites,
In the deep calm, I find my sights.
Awake in love, my heart does sing,
In the embrace of shadows, I take wing.

So let the night unfold its song,
For in this space, I know I belong.
With open arms, I greet the dark,
In the embrace of shadows, I find my spark.

The Freedom Found in Faith

In quiet whispers, shadows fade,
Hearts unbound in grace displayed.
A journey starts with every prayer,
With faith as wings, we learn to dare.

Through trials vast and tempest's roar,
Our spirits soar, forevermore.
In love's embrace, we find our place,
A sacred bond, a holy space.

Each step we take, we lean on truth,
In innocence, we find our youth.
With open hands, we welcome light,
In darkness's depth, we seek what's right.

The burdens lift, the soul is free,
In faith's sweet arms, we cease to flee.
With every dawn, a chance to grow,
In love's pure heart, we come to know.

And so we rise, unchained, awake,
In freedom found, we will not break.
With joyful songs, our spirits shine,
In faith's embrace, our paths align.

Reverence in the Unraveling

When threads of doubt begin to fray,
We seek the light to guide our way.
In moments dark, we bow and breathe,
A love unveiled, we choose to see.

The tapestry of life unfolds,
In silent strength, a truth so bold.
As shadows dance, we stand in grace,
In the unraveling, we find our place.

Each tear we shed, a sacred space,
In pain's embrace, we feel His face.
An offering made, our hearts unbind,
In reverence deep, we seek and find.

With every loss, a chance to grow,
In life's grand weave, we learn to sow.
The beauty found in broken seams,
Awakens spirit, fuels our dreams.

So let us walk in tender care,
Through life's sweet fog, together share.
In reverence, we softly dwell,
Unraveling, we learn to tell.

The Abandonment to Divine Will

In humble hearts, we lay our fears,
To trust the path that love endears.
With open arms, we welcome grace,
In divine will, we find our place.

The whispers soft, our souls align,
In every choice, the stars will shine.
With every breath, surrender flows,
In yielding hearts, true courage grows.

Through winding roads, we learn to roam,
In letting go, we find our home.
The plans we make, in hands unseen,
A dance of fate, a sacred dream.

In storms that rise, we find the calm,
In trials faced, we feel the balm.
For in abandonment, we rise,
Into the vast, we touch the skies.

So here we stand, with faith so bright,
In every shadow, we seek the light.
With God beside, we forge ahead,
In divine will, our spirits fed.

Trusting the Sacred Flow

In every tide, a rhythm found,
The heartbeats echo, love unbound.
We flow like rivers, soft and true,
In sacred trust, we start anew.

With gentle eyes, we watch the days,
In sunlit paths and whispering ways.
For in the ebb and flow of grace,
We dance to life at God's embrace.

Each moment lived, a gift bestowed,
In trust we walk, our fears erode.
With open hearts and willing hands,
Together we weave, as fate commands.

For every twist, the lessons show,
In trusting flow, our spirits grow.
The sacred hymn of life resounds,
In every pulse, love knows no bounds.

So let us brave the currents wide,
In faith we'll sail, never to hide.
By trusting love, we'll find our way,
In sacred flow, we live each day.

Wings of Abandon

In the stillness of the night,
Whispers of grace take flight,
Soaring high on faith's embrace,
Finding peace in sacred space.

With each prayer, my spirit soars,
Leaving behind the heavy doors,
Unfurling wings, I break the chain,
In the light, I feel no pain.

The shadows fade, the dawn arrives,
In trust, my weary heart survives,
Guided by the stars above,
I walk the path of endless love.

In the silence, I hear His call,
Embraced by hope, I rise and fall,
With every breath, I find my way,
In the arms of grace, I stay.

Casting burdens to the wind,
In His mercy, I ascend,
With wings of faith, I leave behind,
The weight that once confined my mind.

The Path to Liberation

With every step, I seek the light,
Through humble hearts, faith takes flight,
A journey marked by love's sweet hand,
In unity, together we stand.

The chains of doubt begin to break,
With every choice, I further wake,
In surrender, I find my strength,
Walking the path, a trusted length.

Through trials faced, I rise anew,
In the storm, there's peace in view,
The dawn of hope begins to shine,
Guided by love's eternal sign.

Faith's embrace softens the fall,
In the silence, I hear His call,
With every tear, a lesson learned,
The heart ignites, the candle burned.

Liberation found in grace,
In His presence, I find my place,
With joy, I walk this sacred road,
In faith and love, my spirit flowed.

A Heart Set Free

In the quiet, I hear His voice,
A gentle whisper, a holy choice,
With every prayer, I let go pain,
A heart set free, I break the chain.

For in the light of purest grace,
I find my truth, my resting place,
In kindness shared, blessings unfold,
A story of love, forever told.

Each moment brings a chance to grow,
In surrender, my spirit glows,
With faith as my guiding star,
I journey forth, no distance far.

When shadows fall, I raise my hands,
And trust in ways I can't understand,
For in the void, His light awakes,
Through heartfelt love, the darkness breaks.

A heart set free, I dance and sing,
In His embrace, I feel the spring,
With open arms and radiant soul,
In love's embrace, I am made whole.

Unburdened by the World

As dawn unfolds with light divine,
I cast away what feels malign,
In the stillness, my spirit sings,
Unburdened now, I spread my wings.

With gratitude, I breathe in peace,
Each moment brings a sweet release,
In every thought, I find the way,
To live in grace, through night and day.

The weight of doubt no longer stays,
In faith, I walk through life's long maze,
With every step, I'm closer still,
To the joy of love, a sacred thrill.

In the simple things, I find delight,
In His presence, the world feels right,
With open heart and tender care,
I find the love that's always there.

Unburdened by the trials faced,
Each day begins with light embraced,
In harmony, I choose to be,
A soul renewed, forever free.

The Path of Holy Release

In silence, I seek His grace,
The burdens of life, I face.
With every step, I find my way,
In faith, I trust, come what may.

Winds of doubt may shake my soul,
Yet His light makes me whole.
I lift my hopes, my prayers soar,
In His arms, I am restored.

The river flows, a sacred stream,
Washing away my darkest dream.
As I release my earthly ties,
I rise to meet the open skies.

With every breath, a new beginning,
The joy of living, ever spinning.
I walk this path, the holy guide,
With every heartache, He's by my side.

Through valleys low and mountains high,
His love surrounds, I cannot deny.
In holy release, my spirit gleams,
A tapestry woven of divine dreams.

Unfurling in Divine Love

In the quiet of the twilight hour,
I feel His gentle power.
With arms wide open, I receive,
In His love, I truly believe.

Petals of faith begin to bloom,
Dispelling shadows, lifting gloom.
In every heartbeat, love does sing,
A symphony of the sacred spring.

As dawn breaks with a golden hue,
I sense the breeze of something new.
Each moment is a gift divine,
In this journey, I intertwine.

The stars above, they whisper low,
Of mysteries only love can show.
I trust the path, His guiding glow,
As in His light, I continue to grow.

Unfurling petals, open wide,
With every tear, He's by my side.
In love's embrace, my heart finds peace,
In pure devotion, I find release.

A Testament of Trust

In shadows deep, I cling to faith,
A spirit strong, a sacred wraith.
With each trial, my heart does yearn,
For lessons learned, and wisdom earned.

He whispers softly in the night,
A beacon in the dark, His light.
Trusting the journey, come what may,
In His promise, I find my way.

Mountains loom, and rivers rage,
Yet in my heart, I turn the page.
Through storms that howl, I shall endure,
My hope in Him remains my cure.

In every doubt, I seek to find,
A testament of love, divine.
For in His arms, I find my rest,
A sacred bond, forever blessed.

With open hands, I give my all,
In every rise, in every fall.
For trust is faith, and faith is light,
My spirit soars, embracing the night.

Embracing the Unknown

In the depths where shadows lie,
I cast my fears, I lift my sigh.
With open heart, I choose to see,
The beauty of what's yet to be.

Each step I take, I may not know,
Yet in His grace, I feel the flow.
Uncertain roads, a call to trust,
In every moment, love is a must.

The unseen paths, they twist and turn,
For wisdom gained, I yearn and yearn.
In the embrace of mystery,
I find the spark of history.

With every breath, I welcome peace,
Embracing change, I feel release.
For in the unknown, His voice I hear,
Guiding my heart, dispelling fear.

So hand in hand, we walk this way,
With every dawn, a brand-new day.
In faith, I rise, my spirit flies,
Embracing the unknown, my heart replies.

From Chains to Wings

In shadows deep, my spirit lay,
Bound by fears in night's cruel sway.
Yet light broke forth, a gentle call,
To rise anew, to break the thrall.

With faith like wind beneath my flight,
I shed the chains, embrace the light.
Limitless love, I find in grace,
Transcendence blooms in every space.

The heart now dances, free from strife,
Through trials learned, I claim my life.
Heaven's whispers guide my way,
From chains released, I soar today.

In every prayer, the starlight beams,
A tapestry of sacred dreams.
Wings of hope on temple air,
In sacred trust, I find my care.

So let my burdens fade away,
With each new dawn, my spirit sways.
In fields of faith, I rise and sing,
From chains of night, to wings of spring.

The Beauty of the Untethered

In fields of grace, where souls are free,
The wild flowers sway, a harmony.
No chains to bind, nor fears to bear,
In breath divine, I find my prayer.

Each moment blooms with colors bright,
In every heart, there burns a light.
Untethered dreams take flight anew,
In sacred trust, we will pursue.

The sky above, a canvas wide,
Where love and hope in peace abide.
With hands outstretched, we rise and soar,
In unity, our spirits pour.

The whispers soft, of ancient lore,
Guide us onward, forevermore.
Together we walk, through life's sweet grace,
In endless love, we find our place.

Each step we take, with purpose clear,
In every heart, the joy we steer.
The beauty found in souls set free,
In harmony, we claim our glee.

So let us dance on this sacred ground,
In unity's song, our hearts are found.
The beauty of the untethered soul,
In love's embrace, we are made whole.

Serenity in the Sweet Surrender

In quiet moments, hearts align,
A gentle touch, the soul's design.
In sweet surrender, peace we find,
A whispered grace, the ties that bind.

The river flows, so calm and clear,
With every wave, I shed my fear.
Through trials faced and burdens shared,
In faith's embrace, we are prepared.

With open hearts, we trust the way,
In darkest nights, we find the day.
Serenity wraps us in its wings,
In softest notes, the spirit sings.

Let go the past, the weight we knew,
In present grace, our strength renew.
The sweet surrender, love divine,
In unity, our souls entwine.

In silent prayer, the truth unfolds,
A sacred hush, where hope upholds.
With every breath, in love we stand,
In sweet surrender, hand in hand.

Together we rise, forever blessed,
In perfect trust, our hearts find rest.
Serenity flows, a river wide,
In sweet surrender, we abide.

The Divine Weaver's Gift

In threads of gold, the weaver spins,
A tapestry where life begins.
Each knot a tale, each color bright,
In woven love, our souls take flight.

The patterns twist, in sacred dance,
A cosmic brush, our hearts' romance.
In shadows cast, the light will gleam,
The weaver's art, a living dream.

From sorrow's loom, the joy will rise,
In every tear, a new sunrise.
With hands of grace, the fibers bind,
The sacred truth, in love we find.

Each life, a thread in greater scheme,
Together woven, a vibrant dream.
The divine weaver, with gentle hands,
Unfolds the heart where peace still stands.

In love's embrace, our spirits soar,
As we're entwined forever more.
Each vibrant strand, a holy lift,
In grateful praise, we share the gift.

So let us honor the weaver's art,
In every stitch, we find our part.
Through trials faced, each journey's grace,
The divine weaver's love, our place.

Ascending through the Release

In the silence, spirits soar,
Heaven's whispers beckon more.
As burdens fall like autumn leaves,
In surrender, the heart believes.

With each prayer, the weight grows light,
Wings of faith take joyful flight.
In love's embrace, we find our way,
To brighter dawns of sacred day.

Let go the chains that bind the soul,
In unity, we are made whole.
In every loss, a greater gain,
Our spirits rise through joy and pain.

From shadows deep, to light above,
We journey forth, guided by love.
Through the release, we learn to stand,
Hand in hand, in His grand plan.

In peace we rest, in faith we rise,
With grateful hearts, we touch the skies.
In every sigh, a prayer flows free,
In surrender, we find our plea.

Echoes of Surrender

In the stillness, souls awake,
Tender whispers, faith we make.
As we bow and let it go,
Divine love begins to flow.

With every heartbeat, we release,
The burdens aching for our peace.
Trust the path laid out with care,
In the void, His light will share.

In silent moments, grace abounds,
Through trials faced, love resounds.
Embracing now, the perfect plan,
In yielding, we become His hands.

The echoes call from realms above,
Guiding us with endless love.
In every fall, we rise anew,
Surrendered hearts, forever true.

Let faith's soft echo fill the air,
In trust, we find Him everywhere.
Through surrender's gentle art,
We journey deep, no fear, no part.

Divine Release

In shadows cast, the light breaks through,
A sacred dance of hope anew.
With open arms, we trust the way,
In divine release, we choose to stay.

Each tear that falls, a prayer of grace,
In every loss, a sacred space.
In letting go, we find our home,
In weary hearts, the light has come.

Through trials faced, we rise to see,
The beauty found in 'set us free.'
In every breath, our spirits sing,
In the embrace of love, we cling.

With every dawn, we find a gift,
In every moment, spirits lift.
In the rhythm of our sighs,
We trust the path our heart defies.

Divine release, our souls take flight,
In unity, we find the light.
As we journey, hand in hand,
God's love, our eternal strand.

Sacred Unraveling

In the depths of heart and soul,
A sacred thread begins to roll.
Unraveling fears, we find our peace,
In the stillness, our worries cease.

With each challenge, we learn to grow,
Trusting the light that guides us slow.
In the unraveling, truth is found,
In every heartbeat, love resounds.

Sacred whispers from above,
Echoing the pulse of love.
In every twist, a chance to learn,
With open hearts, we take our turn.

As we soften to the grace,
In vulnerability, we find place.
Together in this sacred quest,
We find in love our truest rest.

So let us weave in gentle trust,
In sacred paths, in love, we must.
Unraveling the ties that bind,
In faith, our hearts and souls aligned.

Milton Keynes UK
Ingram Content Group UK Ltd.
UKHW020043271124
451585UK00012B/1029

9 789916 897041